SAY NO TO

PLASTIC

101 Easy Ways
to Use Less Plastic

Harriet Dyer

summersdale

SAY NO TO PLASTIC

Text by Abi McMahon

An Hachette UK Company
www.hachette.co.uk

Summersdale Publishers Ltd
Part of Octopus Publishing Group Limited
Carmelite House
50 Victoria Embankment
LONDON
EC4Y 0DZ
UK

www.summersdale.com

Printed and bound in Malta

ISBN: 978-1-78685-821-4

Substantial discounts on bulk quantities of Summersdale books are available to corporations, professional associations and other organisations. For details contact general enquiries: telephone: +44 (0) 1243 771107 or email: enquiries@summersdale.com.

CONTENTS

WHAT'S SO BAD ABOUT PLASTIC?

INTRODUCTION

If you're reading this then it's likely that you want to cut down on your plastic consumption but just don't know where to start. After all, plastic is everywhere! The good news is that it's easier than you think. In this book, you will find 101 little changes that can make a difference. Simply pick one, such as replacing your shampoo with solid shampoo or only buying loose vegetables, and try it for a week. If it works, try it for a month and then add another idea, building on your success. If you're finding that particular idea tricky, pick another.

This book focuses on helping you use less plastic. For that reason, it doesn't explore other eco-friendly factors, such as the carbon footprint from creating other materials. If you're interested in finding out more about that, there are lots of resources online. Successfully tackling our overuse of plastic in our everyday lives can be boiled down to the three main recycling principles: reduce, reuse and recycle. Almost all of the tips in this book teach you how to find second and third purposes for single-use plastics, how to appropriately recycle plastic and how to make better choices in order to reduce your plastic use.

We know that your life is busy, so we've added extra information to each tip to help you decide whether this plastic-reduction method is the best one for your lifestyle. You'll see little icons on each page. This is what they mean:

KEY

This is cheaper than the plastic-based alternative	This option is widely available on the high street	This is a do-it-yourself option
This option reduces the total plastic you use	This option is plastic-free	This option extends the life of your plastic
This option involves donating money	This option involves donating your time	This option involves a new way to do things

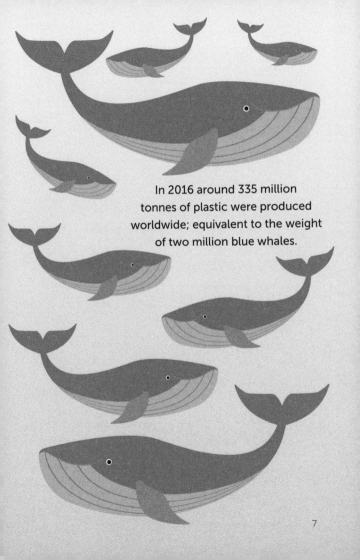

In 2016 around 335 million tonnes of plastic were produced worldwide; equivalent to the weight of two million blue whales.

BIODEGRADABILITY TIMELINE

5 days–1 month	VEGETABLES
2–5 months	PAPER
6 months	COTTON T-SHIRT
1–5 years	WOOL SOCKS
25–40 years	LEATHER SHOES
30–40 years	NYLON FABRIC
50–100 years	TIN CANS
80–100 years	ALUMINIUM CANS
500 years to forever	STYROFOAM CUP
500 years to forever	PLASTIC BAGS
1 million years	GLASS BOTTLES

ENOUGH PLASTIC ENTERS LANDFILL EACH YEAR TO CIRCLE THE WORLD FOUR TIMES.

TEN PER CENT OF ALL WASTE IS PLASTIC.

EVERY YEAR OVER ONE MILLION TONNES OF PLASTIC END UP IN UK LANDFILL, AND IN THE US THE FIGURE IS A WHOPPING 28.9 MILLION TONNES.

EIGHT PER CENT OF THE OIL PRODUCTION WORLDWIDE IS USED TO MANUFACTURE PLASTIC, SO AS WE HEAD TOWARDS 'PEAK OIL' WE CANNOT CONSIDER PLASTIC A SUSTAINABLE MATERIAL.

Around eight million metric
tonnes of plastic ends up
in the ocean every year.

Litter in the ocean is responsible
for the deaths of around one
hundred thousand marine
mammals every year.

In addition to marine
mammals, around one million
sea birds die every year as
a result of ocean debris.

Nurdles are tiny plastic pellets that all plastic products start life as. They often fall into the sea from container ships, creating widespread ocean litter, and are found on 73 per cent of UK beaches. A study in Orange County, USA, found them to be the most common beach contaminant. They do not decompose, but simply break into smaller pieces, and are often eaten by marine wildlife with damaging effects. They're so tiny that they are near impossible to clean from the oceans once they are in there.

It's not just the environment that can be harmed by plastic. Plastic is a processed combination of chemicals, with some plastics containing toxic or carcinogenic (cancer-causing) chemical compounds. Although plastic is slow to biodegrade, exposure to the sun and air can cause some plastics to degrade slightly, 'leaching' hazardous substances into the earth or water around it. If humans come into contact with these substances, by taking a drink from a plastic bottle that's been sitting in the sun for example, they could be exposed to the chemicals.

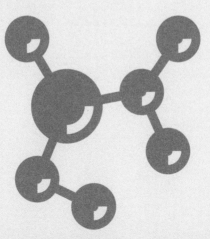

The first step to reducing plastic is knowing what you can recycle and reuse. Here is a quick guide to the common types of plastic:

- **PET or PETE (Polyethylene terephthalate)** – mainly clear drinks bottles and some food packaging. Recyclable but not reusable.

- **HDPE (High-density polyethylene)** – bottles used for things like milk, washing-up liquid and cosmetics. Recyclable and reusable.

- **PVC (Polyvinyl chloride)** – clear food wrapping, shower curtains, toys. Difficult to recycle.

- **LDPE (Low-density polyethylene)** – bags to package bread, carrier bags, squeezable bottles, four-/six-pack can holders. Currently difficult to recycle, although plans are in place to try to change this. A number of supermarkets take carrier bags for recycling.

- **PP (Polypropylene)** – cereal bags, bottle tops, margarine tubs, crisp bags, straws. Reusable and occasionally recyclable, for example, cereal bags and margarine tubs can be recycled.

- **PS (Polystyrene)** – packaging for fragile objects, take-away cups. Not reusable and currently difficult to recycle, although plans are in place to try to change this.

- **Other** – plastics such as acrylic glass, nylon, polycarbonate and items made of a mixture of plastics. Not reusable and difficult to recycle.

PERSONAL
PLASTICS

INTRODUCTION

A really great way to start tackling your plastic usage is to look at the items you use in your daily routines, such as hair conditioner and toothpaste. Because you use them most days, these items generate a lot of regular plastic waste. You'll be surprised by how many alternatives are readily and cheaply available on the high street.

1

SOLID SHAMPOO AND CONDITIONER

Shampoo and conditioner are bathroom items that are used almost daily by most people. This means they get regularly used up and replaced, resulting in countless plastic bottles going in the bin. Try replacing your bottled hair care products with solid shampoo and conditioner. These blocks are often packaging-free or wrapped in paper or card, and are easily available online or in high-street shops, including big chains such as Lush. There are plenty of solid shampoos and conditioners that target hair with 'special needs', such as dry, thin or oily hair, so you don't have to sacrifice great hair in order to save the planet.

2

SOAP BARS INSTEAD OF SHOWER GEL

Replacing liquid hand soap and shower gel with solid bars of soap should be one of the easiest changes in this book. After all, many of us likely use one or the other already. You may be helping to cut down plastic usage without even knowing it. There are a great number of solid soaps already available in supermarkets, from fragrance-free bars for sensitive skin to designer soaps for those who like a bit of luxury. Unlike packaged liquid soaps, soap bars do make a bit of mess so a little stone or ceramic tray can help cut down on cleaning.

3

CANCEL MICROBEADS AND MICROPLASTICS

Microbeads and microplastics are pieces of plastic smaller than 5 mm. They are non-biodegradable and are found in many bath, shower and cosmetics products. As of 2018, the use of microbeads in 'rinse-off' products such as exfoliating scrubs and toothpastes is banned in many countries, including the UK, Italy, New Zealand and the US. Despite this, most laws allow for other microplastics in cosmetics such as lipsticks, or in sun creams or detergents. Check the ingredients list for polyethylene (PE), polypropylene (PP), polyethylene terephthalate (PET), polymethyl methacrylate (PMMA), polytetrafluoroethylene (PTFE) and nylon to help you avoid using products featuring microplastics.

4

USE BAMBOO TOOTHBRUSHES

An easy first step to improving your plastic consumption is to check the packaging of your standard toothbrush. Most toothbrush bristles are made of nylon and are not recyclable at all, but many big-brand handles are now made from recyclable plastic. If you would prefer to avoid the carbon footprint involved in plastic production altogether, try bamboo toothbrushes. Available online or in big-name supermarkets such as Waitrose, bamboo toothbrushes are often packaging-free or use cardboard packaging, and are both recyclable and compostable. Most bamboo toothbrushes are nylon but some are fully compostable. Beware if you are vegetarian, vegan or prefer to avoid animal products as these bristles are often pig hair, a by-product of meat production.

5

SWAP TOOTHPASTE TUBES FOR TOOTHPASTE TABS

Toothpaste tubes are made of plastic and are hard to recycle, although the 'pump action' dispensers are more commonly accepted by recycling facilities than squeezable tubes. An alternative to toothpaste tubes is toothpaste tabs. Solid, chewable toothpaste tabs are available in a variety of flavours, and often packaged in cardboard or recyclable plastic. Toothpaste is used so frequently that we consume a large quantity of plastic through replacing our tubes. Swapping to toothpaste tabs can be an effective way to target your plastic consumption.

6

REPLACE RAZOR BLADES INSTEAD OF RAZORS

Disposable razors produce an extraordinary quantity of plastic waste each time they are replaced. Not only are they often packaged in both an outer plastic wrapper and an inner plastic case, their body is also made of plastic. Swap disposable razors for safety razors. The body of the safety razor is metal so you only need to replace the blade, drastically reducing your plastic consumption. The initial cost is higher than that of disposable razors, but replacement blades can be cheap. There are even companies that provide a subscription service to replace your blades on a regular basis so you don't need to be reminded. The razor industry has gone to a great deal of effort to divide their product by gender but rest assured, a safety razor will give an effective shave on any part of anyone's body.

BATH BOMBS AND BUBBLE BARS

Being eco-friendly doesn't mean you have to give up little luxuries. If you're a fan of relaxing in a big bubbly bath you can still enjoy that, while giving up the plastic-packaged liquid bubble baths. Solid, packaging-free bath bombs can add fragrance, nourishment for your skin and a touch of drama to baths, while you can recreate the bubble effects with a bubble bar. It may not be enough to just swap liquid bath products for solid as some bars are over-packaged and wrapped in plastic.

8

GIVE UP MAKE-UP WIPES

Make-up wipes seem like a convenient method of removing make-up, but they generate a lot of waste. They are less efficient than liquid make-up remover and cotton wool, so they generate waste more regularly. Plus, not all make-up wipes are biodegradable, so many wipes end up piling up in landfills or clogging sewers. You can go one step further than using liquid make-up remover and cotton wool in order to cut your plastic consumption and replace the cotton wool with flannel or reusable cotton rounds. It will require a little extra upkeep, as you will need to wash the flannel or rounds between uses, but you'll cut out even more plastic packaging.

9

USE COCONUT OIL TO REMOVE MAKE-UP

Sometimes using a plastic-packaged item is unavoidable, but you can still make the most of the situation. Rather than buy a bottle of cooking oil and a bottle of make-up remover, buy a big jar of coconut oil. Although most jars of coconut oil are unfortunately plastic, the oil can be used to remove your make-up, to moisturise, as an ingredient in homemade exfoliating scrubs and, what's more, to cook with. That's four plastic bottles in one! Warm a small amount with your hands until liquid, apply to your skin, let sit for a few minutes and then wipe off your make-up with a flannel. Most make-up will come off easily, including waterproof mascara. Coconut oil works well with most skin types although those with oily skin may prefer to avoid it for obvious reasons.

10

BAMBOO COTTON WOOL BUDS

Cotton wool buds with plastic stems are the most common litter found washed up on beaches after being flushed down toilets. There is some action being taken against this by governments and large companies. Scotland has banned the sale of all plastic cotton wool buds, and pharmaceutical company Johnson & Johnson are replacing their plastic stems with paper handles in half the world. You can take action today. Buy cotton buds with bamboo stems and throw used ones on the composter or in your organic waste disposal instead of adding waste to landfills.

11

MAKE YOUR OWN BODY WASHES

You don't have to splash cash on packaging-heavy body washes and exfoliators to have beautiful and healthy skin. You can get great results with many common cupboard ingredients and cut down on plastic waste while you do it. Coconut oil (you can also use castor oil or almond oil) and sugar are the essential ingredients and you can build your scrub from there. Use brown sugar and add cinnamon for a festive scrub, or you could add peppermint extract for a refreshing morning wake-up. If you enjoy the dash of colour body washes bring to your bathroom then mix a few drops of food colouring to your scrubs and display them in glass jars. See p129 for a simple recipe.

12

TRY HENNA HAIR DYE

If you currently dye your hair brown, black or red then you could make a plastic waste 'saving' by switching from liquid hair dye to solid henna blocks. Between the bottles of dye, the dye mixing trays, the applicators and the plastic gloves, home hair dye can result in high production of non-recyclable waste. Blocks of henna are largely packaging-free and are easy to use. There are a few downsides – you still need to wear gloves when applying the dye otherwise you'll stain your hands, and there isn't a large range of colours available, or any options for bottle blondes. But if you like to save the planet and experiment with hair colour, solid henna could be an option for you.

13

TIN LIP BALMS INSTEAD OF TUBES

Lip balms are famously addictive and easy to lose, resulting in the twin troubles of dry, cracked lips and dozens of plastic tubes of balm scattered around your home, only to be thrown away when discovered two years later. Swap your tubes of lip balm to tins of lip balm and at least you'll be able to recycle them when you find them in your old coat pocket. You could even use old tins to carry your coconut oil make-up remover or scrubs in your hand luggage.

14

ECO-FRIENDLY TAMPONS AND TOWELS

As if navigating your period wasn't challenging enough, there's the environmental impact to consider too. Neither plastic nor cardboard tampon applicators are recyclable, and some sanitary towels contain as much plastic as five plastic bags. With half the population in the world using them, that's a lot of plastic waste. Fortunately, there are more eco-friendly options readily available. An easy way to start cutting your sanitary plastic refuse is to use applicator-free tampons, of which there are many brands available in supermarkets. As most big-name sanitary brands have some element of plastic in their cotton mix, whether tampon or towel, look online to find 100 per cent cotton tampons and pads.

15

SUSTAINABLE PERIOD SUPPLIES

There are sanitary products that eliminate single-use plastics. Firstly, you could try using cloth pads or absorbent underwear. There is a larger initial cost with these products but simply pop them in the wash and they're ready to use again. If you are out and about and have a heavier flow then you might need to think ahead, as you can't dispose of the soiled pads or underwear. Another option is a silicone cup that fits inside of you, such as the Mooncup or DivaCup. These can be worn all day, emptied, cleaned and used again, and last for up to ten years. Fitting and changing the cups may take a bit of getting used to, but this is a very eco-friendly method of managing your period.

16

BE ECO-AWARE WHEN HAVING SEX

Sex complicates a lot of things, including people's attempts to live waste-free, plastic-free or even simply in an eco-friendly manner. This book recommends that you always prioritise your and your partner's sexual health and contraceptive wishes when making eco-friendly choices. That said, there are ways to reduce plastic consumption in your sex life. Lube and condoms come in non-recyclable plastic packaging so buying in bulk can shave down the amount of waste you produce. As for condoms themselves, you can get plastic-free condoms in the form of lambskin (how very historical!). However, these only act as a contraceptive and not as a shield against sexually transmitted diseases, and are certainly not vegan-friendly.

CHOOSE ECO-NAPPIES

Newborn babies require around 12 nappy changes a day, which, if you're using disposable nappies, is a lot of plastic going into landfill. Around three billion nappies are thrown away per year in the UK. There are two ways to tackle this problem: biodegradable nappies and cloth nappies. Biodegradable nappies are more expensive than standard nappies, however, some are fully compostable, relieving the burden on landfill. Cloth nappies have a lifespan of around two and a half years, which makes them a budget choice as well as a plastic-free choice. Some parents find the absorbent qualities of cloth nappies to be lacking, plus rewashing and drying can take up valuable time and mental space. One, the other, or a combination of both may work for you. Even cutting down on disposable nappy usage can help reduce plastic consumption.

18

DOES YOUR SKINCARE COMPANY OFFER REFILLABLES?

Some cosmetics and skincare companies, notably those who market themselves as eco-friendly or 'ethical', use plastic packaging but offer customers incentives to refill their product instead of buying all-new. Some companies even have incentives available for those customers who return their packaging, to be recycled by the company. Taking advantage of these offers can save you money as well as cut down single-use plastic waste. Plus, spending money on eco-friendly companies is a great way to 'vote' with your money and incentivise other big-name companies to offer the same eco opportunities.

INTRODUCTION

Plastic has snuck into our homes and now we might feel that it will take a great effort to break the habit. In fact, making the change to a low-plastic lifestyle is easier than you think. Many of the methods of cleaning and shopping are going back to an old-fashioned, slower and simpler way of life which involves using one product for many purposes, and shopping locally.

19

ALTERNATIVE KITCHEN CLEANERS

Most supermarket aisles stock the same kitchen cleaning products, mostly packaged in bright, narrow plastic bottles, to be used quickly and disposed of fast. You can avoid these if you look around a little to find ways to slow your consumption and make eco-friendly choices for your kitchen cleaning routine. Powdered cleaners such as Borax Substitute come in cardboard boxes and larger quantities than standard kitchen cleaners, which often makes them the eco and budget choice. Not always available in smaller supermarkets, these cleaning products are available in other high-street shops, particularly hardware stores, or online.

20

ALTERNATIVE SCRUBBERS

It's not just the packaging for cleaning products that gets regularly thrown away. While most kitchen cleaning implements aren't single-use plastics, they are often disposed of within three months. If you're looking to reduce plastic waste, buying a bristle brush or sponge brush with replaceable heads can be a simple first step. Or, even better, you could revitalise your scrubbers. Clean and deodorise your kitchen cloths by boiling them on the hob or even zapping them in the microwave. You'll kill the bacteria that are festering inside and delay the need to buy another plastic-packaged pack to a later date. There are also plenty of products available online, such as bamboo bristle brushes. As with toothbrushes, the bristles themselves are plastic and non-recyclable, but the handles and heads are compostable.

21

ALTERNATIVE BATHROOM CLEANERS

As with common kitchen cleaning agents, there are many products for the bathroom on the market, most of which are pretty wasteful in terms of packaging. You can find some good alternatives if you're willing to look elsewhere. Borax Substitute works well throughout the house, not just the kitchen, and should be up to tackling most bathroom mess. If you're worried about hygiene then grandmother's favourite, carbolic soap, often comes packaged with easily recycled materials and has antibacterial properties. Used in hospitals until modern antibacterial gels and sprays came on the scene, carbolic soap can be shaved into warm water and used to clean the entirety of your bathroom and toilet.

22

VINEGAR TOILET CLEANER

Even with diligent cleaning, grime and marks can build up in the toilet bowl. Chemical companies have parlayed this into a reason to buy another type of cleaning product – packaged in plastic, of course. You can avoid spending more money and creating more waste by doubling up on the use of a common household product: white vinegar. Simply pour a couple of teaspoons of vinegar into the water, wait a couple of minutes, then scrub and you should have the same effect or better as chemical cleaners.

23

BAKING SODA

If you like to bake then there's a good chance that you have a pot of baking soda languishing at the back of your cupboard. You may not know that you have a powerful all-purpose cleaner hiding in the shadows. Baking soda can tackle many of the home cleaning challenges for which you've been buying additional cleaning products. Just mix with water and use on greasy or dirty kitchens, mix with vinegar and leave on burnt and built-up trays and utensils, or apply as a paste to lift wine stains or built-up mud. Baking soda is often packaged in non-recyclable plastic but using it can reduce your cleaning product collection from several plastic bottles to one small tub.

24

CATCH MICROFIBRES IN YOUR LAUNDRY

One of the struggles with tackling plastic waste is that much of the issue and negative side-effects are invisible. You might be surprised to know that among the microplastics contributing to ocean litter are tiny synthetic microfibres that enter our water systems every time we wash any clothes made of synthetic material, such as Lycra, spandex or polyester. If you don't feel able to give up synthetic clothing materials, such as exercise gear, then you could buy a bag to wash your clothes in. Not all bags will work so search online for brands specifically designed to catch microfibres. Using the bag doesn't eliminate plastic waste entirely, as you still have to scoop out the fibres and dispose of them in the rubbish, but they do reduce plastic's harmful impact.

25

SORT YOUR WASTE

You may have noticed from several of the tips in this book that tackling harmful plastic waste isn't just about reducing the amount of plastic you use. Directing your plastic waste into the best place can help alleviate some of the environmental burden felt by our rapid consumption of non-biodegradable plastic. The first step is to correctly recycle the plastic that can be recycled – double-check online for your local recycling guidelines as your facilities may take products that surprise you. Secondly, the only thing that should be flushed down the toilet is bodily waste and toilet paper (bin cotton wool buds, face wipes, tampon applicators etc.) to alleviate harmful ocean litter. Finally, search out the hidden plastics in seemingly recyclable materials.

26

SODA CRYSTALS

Targeting your dishwashing habits as a way to reduce your plastic waste can be tricky as there don't appear to be as many brands offering plastic-free packaging, as with other household goods. There are soda crystals available online that use cardboard packaging with a metal 'pouring spout'. As with bicarbonate of soda, these can be used for other household cleaning chores in addition to tackling the dishes. Recyclable-packaged bar soap, as suggested in place of body wash, is another alternative. Simply shave a little into your bowl of hot water, soak your dishes, scrub and rinse.

27

MICROFIBRE CLOTHS

Microfibre cloths are cloths made of millions of tiny fibres. Because the fibre count is so high and because the fibres themselves are so small they are better able to stick to dirt particles than standard cleaning cloths. In fact, they're so good at sticking to dirt that you can clean your house thoroughly using only a microfibre cloth and a small amount of water. This means you can stop using plastic-packaged cleaning chemicals altogether. A word of warning: most microfibre cloths are made using a mix of plastics, so you don't eliminate your plastic use completely. They are very durable, lasting for hundreds of rounds of cleaning, making them a good budget option and cutting down on repeat purchases of plastic-packaged cleaning cloths.

28

ECO-SPONGES

Everyone has their favourite cleaning implement. Perhaps cleaning cloths just don't cut it for you and you much prefer to lather up a sponge and go to work. The most common – and cheapest – sponges are made of plastic, which is bad news for sponge lovers. There is some good news for sponge lovers though: some brands offer sponges made of cellulose, which is all-natural wood fibre. If it's the scourer on top of the sponge that you're after, some natural sponges come topped with a rough section made of dried nut shells.

29

REUSE OLD CLOTHES AND TOOTHBRUSHES

Great news! If you are a household that uses a) clothes and b) toothbrushes then you have a ready source of cleaning cloths and scrubbers. By reusing old household materials, you get twice the use for only one instance of packaging, which is a bargain. Of course, you only buy once too, which makes it a budget option. Old flannel shirts and sheets, worn-out towels, socks and cotton T-shirts all make great cleaning cloths. Old toothbrushes provide the scrubbing power for tough-to-tackle built-up dirt.

30

BEESWAX WRAPS FOR FOOD

Cling film is one of those products that appear to make life much easier but we can actually easily do without. It's a single-use plastic that is found in most homes, and a steady stream of it makes its way to landfill every year. Try using beeswax wraps to replace cling film for covering and sealing food in the fridge or transporting food in your bag. Bees wax wraps are compostable, reusable (after being rinsed in cold water) and many come in attractive colours and patterns. They're as convenient as cling film too – simply warm the wrap with your hands to help it stick to a bowl or plate of food that you want to protect.

31

SILICONE LIDS

Another replacement for cling film is silicone lids. Some are stretchy and made to fit over a variety of pots, bowls and tins, while others are sized to common kitchen items such as baked bean tins. All are reusable after a wash, and a great way to cut out cling film from your kitchen waste.

32

ECO PET LITTER BAGS

Poo is hardly the highlight of any pet-owner's day, and it can be even trickier for the animal-lover looking to reduce their plastic waste. Plastic bags are the favourite method of parcelling up pet poo, but of course this all ends up as fodder for landfill. Dog poo can be disposed of in the appropriate park bins without using a bag with the aid of a 'pooper scooper'. When at home you can simply flush your pup's poo down the toilet. Cat poo, however, should not be flushed down the toilet or added to garden compost as it contains bacteria that are harmful to humans. Instead, consider replacing clay litter with sawdust and scooping your cat's waste into paper bags or newspaper 'cones' before disposing of it in your general waste bin. The waste will still enter landfill but will break down much quicker over the years.

SHOP USING YOUR OWN CLOTH BAGS

Plastic bags have been targeted and identified by many countries as one of the biggest enemies in the war on plastic waste. Fifteen countries in Europe, including Denmark, Italy and the UK, have introduced bans, taxes or charges for companies or consumers who wish to use plastic bags. The 5p per bag charge in the UK has seen a positive effect, with the number of plastic bags found in the sea around the UK reduced by 30 per cent since the introduction of the charge in 2015. Many customers use heavy-duty plastic 'bags for life', but you can further reduce plastic in landfill and the sea by swapping these for cloth tote bags. Stronger and more durable than even heavy plastic bags, they are biodegradable too.

34

BUY LOOSE FRUIT AND VEGETABLES

If you are responsible for grocery shopping then you've probably noticed the rise in seemingly unnecessary packaging for fruit and vegetables. Some packaging apparently helps the consumer, such as shrink wrap on cucumbers, which allows the vegetable to stay fresher for longer. Other packaging, such as plastic netting for onion or garlic, or bags for portions of ginger, help the supermarkets by creating pre-weighed or sorted products for which they can charge more. If you compare the price of loose fruit and veg per kilo to packaged fruit and veg per kilo, you'll often find the loose option considerably cheaper. Cut the packaging and the price of your weekly shop and opt for loose fruit and vegetables every time!

35

SWAP PLASTIC BOTTLES FOR CANS

If you like a fizzy drink then you'll likely be pleased to know that most plastic bottles are recyclable. People simply aren't putting their plastic bottles in the recycling bin; it's estimated that up to 70 per cent of plastic bottles go to landfill. The first step to saying no to plastic is ensuring all your plastic bottles make it to the recycling bin, even the ones you buy when you're out and about. An even better option is to stop buying fizzy drinks in plastic bottles and opt for cans. Unfortunately, bulk sets of cans are often wrapped in plastic, but single cans use only aluminium packaging, which is a great recyclable material. Buying cans will likely help you cut your fizzy drink consumption, something your health and your dentist will thank you for.

36

BIODEGRADABLE TEA BAGS

Bad news, tea drinkers! It seems there has been secret plastic in our tea bags for years. Most tea brands use a type of plastic, polypropylene, to seal the bags. While most of the bag will erode away with time, the plastic will linger in landfill. You can search online for a list of tea brands that don't use plastic in their bags, and some supermarket own brands are also plastic-free, such as Waitrose and Aldi. Alternatively, you can buy loose leaf tea and use tea infusers, or a pot and strainer.

37

SAY NO TO COFFEE PODS

There is even worse news for coffee drinkers. Unfortunately for the eco-friendly coffee-lover, pod coffee is out the window. Coffee pods that are used in home machines are made with a combination of aluminium and plastic. With a rate of around one pod per coffee, that's a lot of plastic headed for landfill. If you love good-quality coffee at home, buy a cafetière or a percolator and brew yourself a delicious pot without the plastic waste. If it's variety you need then there are coffee machines that can steam milk and create fancier coffees such as cappuccinos and lattes, using only coffee beans instead of pods.

38

SAY NO TO MICROWAVE READY MEALS

Microwave meals come under a lot of fire for being unhealthy, and unfortunately there isn't much good to say about them in the plastic arena either. Often packaged in a plastic container, covered in a non-recyclable plastic film and enclosed in a laminated cardboard sleeve, microwave meals take a heavy plastic toll. If you rely on them for work, consider cooking up a big batch of reheatable food, such as chilli or a pasta bake, and taking it to work in a microwavable container.

39

CHOOSE FRESH FROM THE BAKERY

Bread is a staple of most households, and consumers tend to buy it off-the-shelf instead of from the bakery. Going back to the bakery is greener – and easier – than you might think. The plastic sleeve and tie that keep supermarket bread fresh contribute to the plastic in landfill, while fresh bread from the bakery is usually wrapped in recyclable paper bags (although some come with clear plastic panels). Modern bakeries offer a wide range of breads and rolls, meaning you won't lose out on choice by switching, and most large supermarkets contain their own bakery, so you don't have to go out of your way to choose the greener option.

40

INVEST IN SOAP BERRIES OR 'WASH NUTS'

Soap berries, or 'Indian wash nuts', have been used for thousands of years as a natural washing detergent by people native to both Asia and the Americas. They grow on trees of the *Sapindus* genus and are a source of saponin, a natural surfactant, which cleans and freshens your clothes. Soap nuts are gentle on your clothes, colours stay brighter for longer, while effectively removing dirt. Available online and in some alternative stores, these eco-friendly scrubbers are often packaged in cloth bags, cutting all plastic from the washing process.

41

ALTERNATIVE SHOPS AND MARKETS

It can be hard to cut down on plastic packaging when faced with aisles of the stuff in supermarkets. Supermarkets have grown to be our main destination for food shopping due to the convenience of having everything under one roof. It's not so convenient, however, if you're picking through the aisles, searching for products that won't add to your pile of plastic waste. Traditional grocers, butchers and weekly markets often offer the same fare – fruit, vegetables, meat, fish and cheese – but without all the packaging. Consider changing your shopping habits and giving up the supermarket for a month to see if you reduce your plastic consumption.

42

BULK BUYING

It takes a little bit of extra money upfront and some forethought, but buying in bulk works well to cut both costs and plastic waste. For example, one big bag of pasta uses less plastic and less processing to make than two small bags of pasta and usually costs less too. This trick won't eliminate your plastic use, but it will help you cut down on those essentials that you haven't found a plastic-free alternative for and can't live without.

43

MAKE YOUR OWN

Making your own combines a few of the plastic-reduction tips already mentioned in this book. Many processed foods come heavily packaged and are a one-and-done product, sending that plastic straight to the landfill. Meanwhile you can bulk buy pasta and purchase loose garlic, tomato and basil to make yourself several easy meals for half the cost and a fraction of the plastic than if you'd bought a bundle of microwave meals. The same goes for sweet treats – flour, sugar, butter and eggs can all be bought in recyclable packaging, and one pack of each is enough to make several cakes.

ON THE GO

INTRODUCTION

For all its many downsides, there's a reason plastic has become so commonly used in our daily lives: it's a cheap, light and sturdy material. In fact, it's perfect for our busy modern world, where we find ourselves short on time and money. This is never more evident than when we're on the go. When you're rushing from one place to another it's so convenient to grab a quick bite to take with you, a bottle of water to keep you hydrated on your journey and maybe even a little treat. A few coins later and you have a whole bagful of plastic that will probably go in the nearest public bin, or a recycling point if there's one available and you have time. These are tough habits to break, but this chapter will target all the ways we create plastic waste when out and about, and suggest easy, and often cheaper, alternatives.

44

PACKED LUNCH INSTEAD OF A SHOP LUNCH

The number of express supermarkets and chain cafés makes it easy to pop out in your lunch hour and pick up a wrap or a toastie. However, at £4 a pop, it's not very economical, and with plastic wrapping and plastic inlays it's certainly not eco-friendly. Bring your own packed lunch to work and you'll eat more healthily, save money, spend less time queuing and create less plastic waste. You don't have to stick to boring sandwiches either – it's relatively quick to cook up a big batch of fajita wrap fillings for the week or mix a variety of seasonal salad.

45

BAMBOO LUNCHBOXES

Reusable plastic lunch boxes are more eco-friendly than single-use sandwich or salad packaging but bamboo lunch boxes are even better. Bamboo is a fast-growing crop whose end product is light, durable and fully compostable, so it's a great resource for those looking to replace plastic completely. Bamboo lunch boxes are readily available on the high street and online and come in a variety of colours, shapes and designs, so whether you're packing sandwiches, salads, leftovers or soups, you're covered.

46

SALADS IN JARS

Glass jars are another alternative to plastic lunchboxes. While they aren't as light as bamboo, they're perfect for those who like their food to look aesthetically pleasing. Plus, glass jars are even more widely available than bamboo lunchboxes and are incredibly durable – it's a one-and-done purchase. If you enjoy experimenting with your lunches there are an abundance of recipes available online and on social media, including burrito bowls, seasonal salads and even homemade instant noodle cups.

47

SAY NO TO STRAWS

If you go out for lunch, it's pretty likely that you'll be getting a soft drink. Most food places like to add 'value' to their soft drinks by providing or offering a straw. However, this little extra comes at a large cost for the environment. In the UK alone, eight and a half billion straws are disposed of each year, but the good news is that a recent awareness-raising campaign on the issue has led to many businesses trying to offer paper alternatives. In the US, a staggering 500 million straws are thrown away each day. However, the anti-straw movement is gaining momentum there too – big companies are making the move to eliminate straws. If you don't need a straw to help you drink, and only the plastic variety is available, simply say no when offered one and you'll make a considerable plastic saving.

48

CARRY METAL OR PAPER STRAWS

As more businesses are becoming aware of the negative impact of plastic straws, some are now offering paper straws as a fully compostable alternative. If you love drinking with a straw, or need one, then this is an eco-friendly alternative to plastic straws. You can even go a step further and carry with you a metal straw, or a handful of paper straws, when you're out and about. Simply remember to wash your metal straw at the end of the day, like you would your lunchbox, and you'll always have a straw on hand. Think of it as a straw for life!

49

CARRY REUSABLE UTENSILS

Supermarkets and cafés often provide plastic utensils so you can eat your food on the go, either included in the packaging or available by the till as a freebie. In principle, this is a handy provision, but in practice you swap about five minutes of forethought for a single-use plastic item that lingers in landfill for millions of years. Pack your kitchen cutlery wrapped in a sheet of kitchen roll (to protect your bag from the dirty cutlery after use) or a beeswax wrap, or even buy a little cloth bag to protect your utensils. It may take you a few days to get used to packing, unpacking and washing your cutlery, but you'll soon find yourself used to your new routine.

50

BUY SANDWICHES FROM BAKERIES AND CAFÉS

A lot of supermarket sandwiches and salads are heavy on the plastic packaging because they have to last on the shelves for a few days. Bakeries, delicatessens and cafés make most of their food fresh and typically supply a bag or box if you plan to take away, but they often opt for cheaper, recyclable packaging, such as paper bags or cardboard boxes. Swap your supermarket snack for a fresher and more eco-friendly bakery or café option – not only do you have an instant non-plastic win, but you're supporting independents too.

51

EAT ICE CREAM OUT OF A CONE INSTEAD OF A TUB

Environmental dilemmas can pop up in the most unlikely of places. You may not have taken the environment into consideration when choosing between ice cream in a cone or a tub, but these summer treats are surprising generators of plastic waste. Opt for a cup of ice cream and you may be served with a plastic tub and a plastic spoon to eat it with – both single-use. So, when faced with that delicious dilemma, choose an ice-cream cone, the eco-friendly option! If you are not a fan of the cone, don't worry, they will happily biodegrade if you put them in a bin.

52

BRING YOUR OWN THERMOS

If you know you're going to be travelling all day and will want a pick-me-up, particularly one containing caffeine, packing your own thermos is a good way to avoid single-use plastics. The plastic lids and part-plastic cups used for takeaway coffee can mount up, especially when you're out and about and not easily able to access a recycling bin. Carrying your own hot beverage also guarantees it will be made how you like it and far cheaper.

53

BRING YOUR OWN REUSABLE BOTTLE OF WATER

Bottled water isn't just a plastic hazard, it's an unnecessary expense too. Water in bottles comes massively marked up in price, even more so if you have limited purchase options, such as in a railway or service station. The average cost of a litre of tap water in the UK is just 1p, compared to 65p for bottled water, while in the US the cost per gallon is $0.004, 300 times cheaper than the bottled price of $1.22. Take your own bottle of water with you when you travel. Many camping and cook stores sell attractive metal flasks in a variety of sizes. Some bottles even have the technology to keep your water cool, so you get the advantage of chilled water on a hot day.

54

PACK READY-MADE SNACKS FOR LONG JOURNEYS

Part of the fun of long journeys, particularly trips in the car, is the little stop-off on the way where you treat yourself to a bar of chocolate or some crisps for the car. Just sticking to toilet stops might not seem as fun, but it's better to avoid accumulating those little piles of plastic wrappers and cartons that come with impulse-bought snacks. Of course, being eco-friendly doesn't mean you have to be healthy! If taking a bag of satsumas with you just won't cut it, make a simple tray bake the day before, such as brownies, or make your own vegetable crisps, and salt away to your heart's content.

55

CHOOSE CARPOOL/ PUBLIC TRANSPORT

You've heard that cars are bad for the environment because of greenhouse gases. You've heard that cars are bad for your health and you should walk more. Well, now we're here to tell you that cars are bad for the environment, and particularly the oceans, because the slow wearing down of tyres produces microplastics that litter our sea. This is a global issue and one that is fairly new to the eco-agenda but, based on the recent research, it deserves a higher place and priority on the political agenda than it currently receives. Carpooling, opting for public transport or walking or biking where you can will help slow the wear of tyres and ease the burden on the oceans.

56

USE REFILLABLE PRODUCTS FOR TRAVEL ABROAD

Due to hand luggage restrictions on flights you might find yourself buying a lot of products that you already own, but in miniature. If you've already read the sections on solid soaps, conditioners and body washes then good news! All of these can be taken on planes in your hand luggage without falling foul of the liquid limit. If you still prefer to take your liquid products then there is an alternative to buying the smaller bottle versions. Purchase a small set of plastic bottles and decant some of your existing product into them. You'll be covered for all of your upcoming holidays instead of using – and discarding – plastic every holiday.

SPECIAL
OCCASIONS

INTRODUCTION

Plastic can rear its ugly head in all sorts of surprising situations. Unfortunately, with most special occasions comes a flurry of spending, decorations and presents, and where there is extra consumption, there is always plastic. Packaging, wrapping and even gifts themselves can really add to the landfill – Christmas in the UK alone brings 450,000 double-decker buses worth of waste. Fortunately, as with many of this book's solutions to using less plastic, the answer lies in planning ahead and making a few simple substitutions.

57

FIND AN ALTERNATIVE TO WRAPPING WITH TAPE

You've heard that sticky tape is plastic-based and not recyclable. However, that doesn't have to mean the end of gift-giving (sorry, Scrooges!). Instead of tape, secure your wrapping with a natural fibre. Plain string or raffia can look quite retro and attractive, especially if you slip a sprig of flowers or a treat alongside the bow. If you love the spectacle of decorated presents there are plenty of alternatives such as coloured wool or twine, silk ribbon or pretty lace, all of which can be used in place of sticky tape.

58

ECO WRAPPING PAPER

Even though it's called wrapping *paper* it's not always recyclable. Sometimes plastic hides itself and tries to trick us. Try the 'scrunch' test – if you scrunch the paper up and it holds, it's recyclable; if it unfolds itself then it's destined for landfill. Glitter, foil and heavily laminated papers are never recyclable, so you don't have to try the scrunch test before you buy. Keep an eye out for how your wrapping paper is wrapped too. You can buy some sheets 'bare' or a roll that's been fastened by a small paper label, but some wrapping paper rolls come shrink-wrapped in plastic. You can even go a step further and buy ready-recycled brown paper, which can look very effective as a wrapping, or go for a DIY approach and get creative by making your own. There's plenty of inspiration online.

59

THINK CAREFULLY ABOUT CARDS

Cards are also tricky as they would seem to be recyclable, but often they contribute to plastic waste. As with wrapping paper, most cards, especially packs such as Christmas cards, are wrapped or housed in plastic packaging. You can avoid this packaging by choosing carefully in high-street shops or buying cards from artists in indie shops and markets. Cards also suffer the same problem of being embellished – glitter, foil and laminate are all sources of non-recyclable plastic. Careful selection, often from alternative shops, can help you avoid this, or you can shop online for eco-cards that not only avoid plastic but also utilise recycled card.

60

NO BALLOONS

It's sad to say but as much joy as balloons bring to parties, they wreak havoc on the environment. Balloons are made of rubber, latex, polychloroprene or nylon and many will have a metallic coating. However, plastic or no plastic, in landfill they either take years or do not biodegrade at all and many end up in the sea, where unsuspecting sea life consume them and are harmed, or even die. If you would like to festoon your home in celebration, opt for cloth bunting.

61

PAPER INSTEAD OF PLASTIC CUPS AND PLATES

While giving ceramic plates to a party full of young and over-excited children might be a recipe for disaster, plastic cups and plates are off the menu. Opt instead for paper plates or even ones made of palm leaf. Remember to avoid laminated paper, as that isn't easily recyclable. Palm leaf is naturally shed, so doesn't contribute to the destruction of palm forests, and the plates are completely compostable (once you've scraped the cake off). Unfortunately, many paper plates come wrapped in plastic packaging, but that's an improvement on plastic wrapped in plastic.

62

USE POPCORN TO PACK FRAGILE ITEMS

We can't always be with our loved ones at their special time but sending them a gift is a great way to share in their special moment. Things get trickier when that gift is fragile and needs to be safely wrapped without using plastic. Polystyrene packing peanuts are made of plastic and are not often recyclable. Replace them with popped popcorn. Popcorn fits as well around a fragile item and will protect it on its journey, plus it's fully compostable. Use plain popcorn, or buy kernels and pop it yourself – you don't want to cover the present with salty or toffee residue!

63

SHOP LOCALLY INSTEAD OF ONLINE

You can control the packing materials in the parcels you send, but you can't control the packing materials in the parcels that are sent to you (yet). Most things you buy online often come wrapped in layers of plastic or are kept safe by bubble wrap or packing peanuts. Shop locally and buy locally made where possible to reduce both your plastic waste and the carbon footprint of your purchase.

64

ECO-TOYS FOR CHILDREN

For little people with very little access to money, children generate a tremendous amount of plastic waste as they love and discard favourite toys. It's easy to see why plastic became the popular choice for children, due to its durability, cheapness and wipe-clean nature. However, it isn't the only option available. Eco-conscious toys made of wood and cloth are available online and in alternative shops. They might be a little pricier but are much kinder to the environment.

PLASTIC
ACTIVISM

INTRODUCTION

Don't worry, the burden of doing something about plastic doesn't rest solely on your shoulders. There are all sorts of groups and initiatives out there that are already working hard to reduce both the creation of plastic and plastic consumption, lobbying to raise awareness and trying to bring the issue of plastic to the attention of the media and the government. Join in with other like-minded people and lend your voice to their cause because we're all in this together.

65

TAKE 3 FOR THE SEA

Take 3 For The Sea is a clean beach initiative aimed at reducing marine waste. Its method is simple: every time you go to the beach, pick up three items of waste and dispose of them when you get home (recycling where possible). Of course, you can also apply this to our increasingly litter-filled countryside and towns. In fact, if you keep a little bag on your person then it's easy to pick up three items of litter whenever you go out.

66

BEACH CLEANS

Many nature-loving societies around the globe run organised beach cleans. Simply look online for ones in your area and you'll be able to join with other like-minded individuals to pick litter and plastic waste from our beaches. Most organised beach cleans provide you with protective gloves and litter pickers, and educate you on how to look for less obvious plastic waste such as nurdles. Of course, you can always do a beach clean on your own or with friends.

67

30-DAY ZERO WASTE CHALLENGE

Going Zero Waste challenges you to go a month without generating any waste for the landfill. You can recycle materials and compost food waste, but you can't add anything to your general waste bin. This doesn't just target plastic, but it's a great way to help you break bad habits and rethink how you consume goods. If you'd like to take on this challenge then there are plenty of useful suggestions in this book that will help you out.

68

CHARITIES – GIVE MONEY

There are lots of charities that are tackling the plastic crisis, many of them marine conservationists or local beach-loving groups. Donating money to these charities can really help them in their battle to reduce plastic. Money is required to buy advertising, stock up on resources, organise events in local areas, create informational materials and much more. This is a great option for people who might feel overwhelmed by the burden of reducing plastic – why not support the experts?

69

CHARITIES – GIVE TIME

All charities need money and most charities also need volunteers. Giving a couple of hours each week to anti-plastic charities can be enormously helpful. They don't have much money available, so it takes people power to support their events, hand out their informational material and fundraise. If you can spare a little time, even to attend their events, then it will go a long way.

70

HOLD A SPONSORED EVENT

Charities benefit greatly from larger cash donations. You don't have to dig deep to find the money yourself – you could hold a sponsored event to generate a few more coins for your charity of choice. Whether you're a baker, an athlete or a hobby car washer, sponsoring a charity does not only raise cash but also awareness for your cause.

71

GO PAPER-FREE WITH MAIL AND CATALOGUES

Those little plastic panels on paper envelopes are stylistic rather than necessary choices and just go directly to landfill. Sit down one evening with your bills and subscriptions and see if you can switch everything over to online access only. It may take a little getting used to – don't forget to pay your credit card because you're waiting for the bill to arrive – but it's a one-and-done way to make a plastic saving.

72

TAKE POLITICAL ACTION

Big changes simply can't be made without governments getting behind them. Large companies are ruled by monetary incentives and won't switch from cheap, money-saving plastic materials unless an equally large entity, such as the government, challenges them, legislates against it or imposes monetary penalties. Writing to a relevant body in power is a good way of raising an issue, and the more of us that do that the more support there will be for governments to support anti-plastic sanctions and legislate against plastic.

73

NAME AND SHAME

For better or for worse, shaming on social media is an effective modern-day campaigning tool. Companies care deeply about their public image, as a good public image means money. Take a snap of a particularly ridiculous piece of over-packaging and express your disappointment and displeasure online. Companies will be tracking perceived problems and sometimes make decisions based on how their customers react to it.

74

ATTEND LOCAL TOWN HALLS, COUNCIL MEETINGS OR Q&As

Most local governments hold regular meetings with the public where hot topics and issues can be raised. For many this is a great way to talk directly to their local representative and be heard on issues that are important to them. Many effective campaigns start at the local level – it's much easier to gain traction once you have people in power on your side. Good local issues to tackle include reducing litter and combating waste in your local area.

75

STOP FLUSHING PLASTIC

The only thing that should be going down your toilet is body waste and toilet paper (you can still flush for those). Wipes, sanitary items and buds all contain plastic and they go directly to the sea when flushed. Although plastic in a landfill isn't ideal, it's better than in the stomach of a marine animal or floating on a 'plasticberg'.

76

COMPOST FOOD WASTE

Every little helps when it comes to plastic reduction. Compost for the garden comes in plastic bags that are rarely recyclable. Buy a compost bin (check with your local authorities to see if your purchase can be subsidised) and dispose of your (uncooked) food waste so that you'll never have to buy another bag of compost again.

77

REPAIR CLOTHES

Some plastic waste is invisible to us in our daily lives. Although you avoid plastic packaging by buying clothes in-store, it is likely (unless the clothes are made locally) that they would have travelled wrapped in swathes of plastic on their way from the factory to the warehouse, and then again from the warehouse to the factory. Maintaining your clothes instead of replacing them when you wear through them will not only save you money but also save on 'invisible' plastic consumption.

EAT AT ZERO-WASTE RESTAURANTS

It's possible to reduce waste in every area of your life, even the fun parts. Restaurants and bars are by their very nature areas of massive consumption and produce a lot of waste, including plastic. Zero-waste restaurants aim to combat this and are popping up all over the place. Many of their products are made on-site and they wring every last use out of their ingredients, so they don't have to buy in as much. Plus, who can resist a tasty dish?

79

DON'T GO IT ALONE

If you've got this far in the book and you're feeling a little overwhelmed, don't be! You don't have to do this alone. There are many online forums and blogs full of like-minded people, sharing new plastic-reduction tips, recipes, ideas and feedback on what works and what doesn't. Local sites can also give tip-offs about events you might like to be involved with and causes you can lend your voice to.

80

SLOW LIVING AND ANTI-CONSUMERISM

So little of our products are made locally now that it's likely almost everything you buy will have travelled a long way to get there, building up a carbon footprint and using a lot of plastic. Making the ethical choice to buy food, clothes and gifts at local shops or markets can help cut the carbon spend and plastic waste. Some have built these choices into a lifestyle movement called 'slow living', claiming that living mindfully, maintaining goods instead of replacing them, and cooking according to the seasons, helps with mental health and well-being as well as the environment.

81

READ UP ON THE BUSINESS POLICIES OF COMPANIES

It's as important to reward good business practice as it is to bring attention to not-so-good business practice. Research your preferred brands and see how they are engaging with plastic policies. It could be that they have some positive policies that make you want to continue giving them money, or perhaps their rival might draw your loyalty. For example, the computer company Dell has recently committed to using only recyclable packaging, and the skincare company Lush has a long-standing packaging-free policy.

82

USE PRIVATE 'RECYCLE EVERYTHING' COMPANIES

What local recycling companies are able to recycle varies from area to area, so how successful you are at recycling your plastic waste may sometimes be dictated by where you live. As an alternative, check online to source private companies such as TerraCycle that offer to take and recycle any waste you may produce. For a fee (that scales up the more you send in) you can package up and submit all your waste, including hard-to-recycle materials.

83

SHOP AT SELF-BRANDED 'ETHICAL SHOPS'

Ethical shops and 'packaging-free' shops are great places to shop when avoiding plastic. Being plastic-free is part of their ethos, so it saves you the effort of checking every product as you shop. They may also feature large containers of dry goods, which are rarely plastic-free in large supermarkets, such as pasta or muesli.

84

BUY IN BULK WITH FRIENDS

You can reduce plastic packaging by buying items in bulk, but you can capitalise on that tactic by teaming up with friends. If a few of you put money in a pot you can buy large amounts of items and split them. This works especially well for deli items such as cheeses or meats as they expire too quickly for one person to buy and store large amounts.

85

INVOLVE YOUR WORKPLACE IN POLICIES

Talk to your boss about introducing eco-friendly work policies into the workplace. Depending on the size of the company, this can have a real impact as the policy could affect many people, and as a result, help to reduce plastic. This could be anything from forming a small group among your colleagues to buy bulk lunch goods, implementing a strong recycling initiative, or even getting the company to agree to change its practices to avoid buying tea bags with plastic, or coffee pods.

UPCYCLE

INTRODUCTION

These crafty ideas are the perfect way to use up hard-to-recycle plastics and avoid buying more plastic tat for the house. If you have children look for the 'great for kids' sticker marking cheap crafts that are perfect for little hands.

86) PLASTIC BOTTLE IRRIGATION SYSTEM

Here's a great way to recycle plastic bottles and enrich your plants at the same time.

You will need: plastic bottle, skewer.

In dry weather, it can be hard for water to get down to the roots of your bigger plants.

Take an empty drinks bottle and pierce holes all over it with a skewer, then bury it next to your plant with the top just poking out above the soil.

Fill the bottle with water and it will gradually be released where your plant needs it most – deep down at its roots.

87) T-SHIRT TOTE BAG

With just a few strategic snips, you can make a stylish, not to mention economical and eco-friendly, tote bag out of an old T-shirt.

You will need: cotton T-shirt, scissors, ruler.

Select a T-shirt. Place the T-shirt flat on a work surface and cut off the sleeves along the shoulder seams.

Turn the T-shirt inside out and place it on the work surface with the bottom seam closest to you.

Arrange the bottom edges so they overlap neatly and cut vertical slits from the bottom all the way along, cutting about 5 cm deep and 3 cm apart. You can use a ruler to keep your cuts even.

Next make a vertical cut along each side seam, also around 5 cm deep.

Working from one side to the other, knot each set of cuts together. Double-knot to create a secure base for your bag.

Turn your new tote bag right side out, and it's ready to use.

88) DIY BEESWAX WRAPS

Beeswax wraps are eco-friendly but a little pricey for some households. Make the most of old sheets and pillow cases by converting them into wraps with this cheap and easy method.

You will need: old (clean) cotton pillow cases or sheets, scissors, a baking sheet, beeswax, paintbrush.

Cut your material down to size. Measure it against the pots and boxes you'll be wrapping in it to see how big it needs to be. If you have a lot of spare material, cut a few sheets of different sizes.

Preheat your oven to 100° centigrade, 200° Fahrenheit. Lay the material flat on the baking sheet.

Grate the beeswax evenly and generously over the sheet. Place in the oven until the wax is melted.

Remove from the oven and use the paintbrush to spread the wax over the material so it is entirely covered.

89) PLASTIC BOTTLE PLANTERS

Utilise small or urban garden spaces by hanging planters down the fences. These are perfect for tumbling tomatoes, strawberries, herbs and salad leaves.

You will need: plastic bottles, string, paint, paint brush, drill, plastic piping or sturdy branch (optional).

Remove the paper or plastic label from the bottle but keep the lid on.

Squash the bottle flat and cut a rectangle from the middle of one side. Pop the bottle back into shape.

Paint your bottle in the colour of your choice. This makes the planter opaque, so the roots won't bleach and be damaged.

Drill a hole through the top and bottom of each side of the planter for threading string to attach them to your fence.

Thread your string through your string holes, knotting it above the top hole and below the bottom so it stays in place.

Fasten the string to a post or a strong branch/plastic piping and your planters are ready.

90) PLASTIC SPOON LAMPSHADES

This is a great hack for used plastic spoons after a big event (but remember to wash them first).

You will need: plastic spoons, large plastic bottle, glue gun, cutting knife, pliers, fixture wire, electrical tape (optional).

Cut a hole in the bottom of your plastic bottle with your cutting knife. Then cut the handles off your spoons, leaving only the heads.

Glue a circle of heads at the base of the bottle, tips facing down and halfway over the edge. Glue a second layer overlapping halfway over the first. Repeat until the whole bottle is covered up to the neck.

Thread the fixture wire through the neck and screw the bulb in from the bottom of the shade. You can cover up the neck according to your style – an overlapping ring of spoon heads looks good, or even some simple black electrical tape looks modern.

91) 'HOT-AIR BALLOON' BOTTLE DECORATIONS

These hot-air balloons are easy crafts and can look surprisingly attractive when strung up. They're great for decorating a child's bedroom or simply as a quick make for a rainy day.

You will need: 2-litre plastic bottle, cutting knife, paint, paint brush, hot glue gun or masking tape.

Remove the paper or plastic label and cut the middle out of the bottle (recycle the excess).

Glue or tape the base and the lid-end together. When hung, lid-end down, this will look like a hot-air balloon.

Use paints to create your balloon effect – large stripes are a great way to make it look like a classic hot-air balloon. Your lid is your basket. You don't need to do anything to this, but you can paint it a bright colour for maximum effect.

GREAT FOR KIDS!

92) PLASTIC BAG WOVEN TABLE MATS

Plastic bag table mats are wipe-clean, hardy and, if you use the right bags, bright and fun. They're a great choice for accident-prone children.

You will need: glue gun, 10+ plastic bags, sharp needle, thread.

Flatten out your plastic bag and cut it into a spiral in order to get as long a strip of plastic as possible. The ideal width for the strips are 4 cm wide. Double over three strips so you have six equal strands and plait together. Tie in a fresh set of strips when you come to the end and continue plaiting, until you have a nice long plait.

Coil your long plait together. Starting from the outside and moving round the coil, sew each row to the next with widely-spaced stiches. Then take your glue gun and glue between the gaps, pressing the layers of coil together as you go for a firm finish.

Turn the coil over and you have a ready-to-go table mat.

93) PLASTIC PIPING TOOL-UTENSIL RACK

If you've been doing a bit of DIY and have a few leftover plastic materials lingering, try making this storage rack using offcuts of plastic piping (think drain piping).

You will need: plastic pipe, two lengths of batten, saw.

How many tools you want to house will determine the length of pipe needed. You'll need two 10-cm lengths for each tool.

Once you've cut your pipe, fix two lengths of batten (2.5 x 5 cm or similar) horizontally to the shed wall, cut wide enough to accommodate all of your tools.

Fix one at just above floor level and the other parallel, about a metre above the first. Attach your pipe pieces evenly across the batten, ensuring they line up vertically.

Now you have a neat and tidy tool rack, enabling you to grab a broom and a rake at a moment's notice.

94) MILK CARTON WATERING CAN

Here's a great way to make the perfect watering can for your plants – and you get to choose how fine a spray your can produces.

You will need: milk carton, heated needle, drill (optional).

Use a large, empty milk container with a screw-on lid and pierce holes in the lid with a heated needle.

Smaller holes will give you a gentle, fine spray – perfect for watering your more delicate blooms without drowning them or damaging their petals.

You can use a drill to make larger holes if you want to water sturdier plants or soak a bigger area.

Once you've created your desired hole size, fill the carton with water, replace the lid and get watering.

95 PLASTIC BOTTLE TOY TIDY

Try this upcycle if you're plagued by tiny toys on the carpet but don't want to pay unnecessary cash for specially designed tidies.

You will need: large plastic bottle, cutting knife, screwdriver, screw.

Cut across the middle of the bottle; if you want a deep toy tidy, cut closer to the lid, but if you only need a shallow tidy, cut close to the base. The cut should be sloped, so you end up with a higher 'back' and a lower 'front' for little hands to reach into.

Turn so the hole is at the top (you'll need to keep the lid on for the top half of the bottle so the toys don't escape) and screw onto the side of your chest of drawers or desk.

You can paint the bottle after cutting it to match it to the colour scheme of your room, or encourage your child to decorate it as a fun activity.

96) PLASTIC BOTTLE SPRINKLER

This upcycle could not be simpler and it certainly saves a journey to the shops when you'd rather be having fun on a hot summer's day.

You will need: plastic bottle, drill or hot needle.

All you need to do to create your sprinkler is to drill or jab several holes in your plastic bottle. Two or three lines of closely-set holes at the end of the bottle works well. Alternatively, several lines spread about the length of the bottle also works.

Thread the hose through the neck of the bottle and turn on the water.

As the sprinkler works by creating water pressure, you may need to secure your hose in place with a little bit of masking or electrical tape. You could also drape the end of the hose over a large rock or block of wood so it is directed down into the bottle.

97) MELT PLASTIC BAGS INTO BEADS

If you are low on cash or resources and still love crafting, this is a great way to salvage something beautiful out of waste.

You will need: clean plastic bags, baking paper, iron, crafting glue, wooden skewers, scissors, ruler.

Cut your plastic bag into 8 cm x 8 cm squares.

Place two squares on top of each other and enclose in baking paper. Set your iron to low heat and press across the area for about 30 seconds. The two bits of plastic should be firmly stuck together to create one piece of smooth material.

Cut your fused squares into long triangles. You can change the width and length of the triangles – longer triangles make fatter beads and wider triangles make longer beads.

Lightly apply glue to one side of the triangle, starting 0.5 cm from the widest part. Then roll the triangle around the skewer, base first, and secure with a further blob of glue.

When dry, slide off the skewer.

98) DIY DISH DETERGENT

You'll find that making your own dish detergent is both cheaper and easier than you first expect. The initial cost of the liquid Castile soap is around £3, and one bottle makes many batches of dish detergent.

You will need: ½ cup liquid Castile soap (an all-natural vegetable oil-based soap easily available online), ½ cup water, 1 teaspoon lemon juice, 3 drops tea tree extract, ¼ cup white vinegar.

Stir the water and liquid soap together.

Add the rest of the lemon juice, tea tree extract and vinegar. Mix until combined.

Transfer into a bottle for storage. Use 2 tablespoons per load.

99) DIY ALL-PURPOSE CLEANER

This recipe combines the king and queen of cleaning: vinegar and bicarbonate of soda. It's less effort than going to the shops too – making this takes less than 5 minutes.

You will need: ½ cup white vinegar, ¼ cup bicarbonate of soda, 2 litres water.

Combine ingredients in a bottle and mix well.

Decant into a spray bottle or add a spray head to the bottle it's already in.

100) DIY BODY SCRUB

All you need to create the base of a scrub is equal parts sugar and coconut oil. You can scale the recipe up or down depending on how much you need or how big your pot is.

You will need: 150 g coconut oil, 150 g sugar, watertight pot.

Mix the sugar and oil in the pot.

Store in the bathroom with the lid on.

101) BOTTLE CAP MOSAIC

This craft is relatively mess-free, a perfect activity to keep creative kids busy with minimal clean-up.

You will need: lots of bottle tops, thick cardboard, glue or sticky tack (optional).

The only limit to this craft is how many lids you have to hand. A wide range of colours is preferable.

If your children need a little bit of guidance, you can sketch out a shape on the cardboard, such as a butterfly or a fish, and have them fill it with bottle lids. Otherwise, let their or your imagination run free.

Because plastic is so durable, it's great to simply lay the mosaic and then pack it all away at the end of the game. If your child wants to create a work of art, then it's simple to glue or tack the lids in place.

If you're interested in finding out more
about our books, find us on Facebook
at **Summersdale Publishers** and
follow us on Twitter at **@Summersdale**.

www.summersdale.com